An Introduction
to Systematic Theology

An Introduction to Systematic Theology

WOLFHART PANNENBERG

WILLIAM B. EERDMANS PUBLISHING COMPANY
GRAND RAPIDS, MICHIGAN

Copyright © 1991 by Wm. B. Eerdmans Publishing Co.
255 Jefferson Ave. S.E., Grand Rapids, Mich. 49503
All rights reserved

Printed in the United States of America

Library of Congress Cataloging-in-Publication Data

Pannenberg, Wolfhart, 1928–
An introduction to systematic theology / Wolfhart
Pannenberg.
p.   cm.
ISBN 0-8028-0546-9
1. Theology, Doctrinal — Introductions.   2. Theology —
Methodology.
I. Title.
BT65.P36   1991
230 — dc20   91-124
CIP

Contents

An Introduction
to Systematic Theology

1

The Need for Systematic Theology

In the history of Christianity, there was always a fundamental question to be faced and to be answered, the question of why an individual person should commit herself or himself to be a member of the Christian church. In the case of a Jew, one is born as a Jew. But one is not born as a Christian — one has to be reborn. Certainly, since the fourth century, baptism in most cases has become a matter of early childhood. The difference from the assumption of being a Christian by birth does not seem tremendous. Nevertheless, the sign of baptism has to be appropriated in the course of one's life. Otherwise, it becomes an empty sign. It is not that the life of a Christian first begins with personal conversion. It does start with baptism, but one's baptism has to be remembered and reappropriated again and again until we die. Thus, being a Christian remains a very personal affair.

There are all sorts of particular reasons and factors in each individual story of becoming a Christian. But in any event one has to become a believer. And Christian belief has always been belief in God and in Jesus Christ. This is what makes a Christian: To confess to Jesus Christ that in him God has been active to restore and reconcile the human race and through the human race his entire creation. Again, there is a significant difference from being a Jew or, say, a Hindu. One is a member of the Jewish or Hindu people by birth. It may be important to confess to the faith of the fathers and to obey the traditional rules of life, but personal confession is not constitutive of being a Jew or a Hindu. In the case of the Christian, his or her personal confession to Christ is constitutive of being a Christian. It is bound up with one's baptism. It is not the only issue in baptism, of course. In our baptism God called our life once and for all, beyond our capacity of answering his call at any particular moment. But still, our confession of faith belongs to the integrity of our baptism. It is only in the personal faith of the individual that our baptism is alive.

The problem that is involved in this situation becomes sharpened when we consider that it is precisely the Jewish God, the God of the Hebrew Bible, whom the Christian believes and confesses to be truly God. What in the world should motivate a person to embrace the God of another nation? We may say it is Jesus and his teaching. But Jesus was a Jew himself, and most Christians are not. To a Jew it may be natural to honor the God of his or her forebears, though even that is not a condition for being a Jew. In the case of the Christian, however, whose background is Gentile and who only becomes a member of the Christian community by confessing to the God of Israel, why should such a person do so?

Here we are at the core of our subject, the need for systematic theology, because it all depends on the question of truth: If we suppose that the God of Israel and of Jesus is the one and only true God, then and only then is there sufficient reason for believing in that God, even if one is not a Jew.

In each personal story of becoming a Christian or of personally appropriating the call that claimed our lives in the event of our baptism, there will be many factors and motives contributing to our involvement in the Christian faith, and many of those factors and motives may be more or less accidental, but all of them, even our most personal experiences, would turn out to be superficial or deceptive if the God whom Jesus proclaimed, the God of Israel, were not the one true God. In being a Christian, everything depends on the reality of God. This explains the fundamental importance not only of belief and dogma but also of theology in the history of the Christian church. We cannot honestly go on to identify ourselves as Christians if the story of Jesus Christ and of his God is merely a story (in the sense of fairy tale) — fiction, but not history. The Christian faith cannot live by relating to the history of Jesus as to a myth of Christian ancestors, if it were just that. The problem with the term "story" is that it obfuscates the truth question, and I suspect that the term "story" is so popular precisely because it allows one to slide over the truth question. The story of Jesus Christ has to be history, not in all its details, but in its core, if the Christian faith is to continue. The same applies to the term "myth": God must be real, not just mythical if we are to entrust ourselves to him.

The question of truth in religion is not only a theological question. It is not even theological in the first place. Before it comes to theology, there is a feeling of reliability or an awareness, but vaguely perceived, of the mysterious reality that encompasses and pervades our lives. To most people, beauty speaks of truth in more powerful ways than any intellectual argument does. Nevertheless, whatever we take as true in experiential immediacy may be challenged. All momentary certainty stands in need of further confirmations and interpretation, and it is only by reference to the unity of all our experience and of all our knowledge that we can determine what is true. Coherence provides the final criterion of truth, and it can serve as such a criterion because it also belongs to the nature of truth: Whatever is true must finally be consistent with all other truth, so that truth is only one, but all-embracing, closely related to the concept of the one God.

Considerations like this belong to the level of reflection, not to the realm of experiential immediacy. It is on the level of reflection that theology is concerned with the truth of the Christian faith. Nevertheless, the Christian experience and the Christian community of faith need the work of theology, because it is on the level of reflection that all claims of truth are to be judged. The missionary proclamation of the Christian church, asserting that the God of Jesus is the one and only true God and that he truly raised Jesus from the dead, entails a need for theological reflection, a need for an examination and confirmation of its truth claims on the level of reflection. If theology properly faces that task, it can be of invaluable help in encouraging the preacher and in strengthening the good conscience of every individual Christian that the teaching of the church is true. If theology does not properly face its particular task regarding the truth claims of the Christian tradition, then it easily happens that the clergy of the church are the first to become insecure and evasive about the message they are supposed to preach. When they become doubtful about the truth of the gospel, they will tend to replace it by other "causes," and the believers will be disturbed, because they no longer get to hear in church what they rightfully expect to be taught there.

The task of theology is not only to investigate the origin

and the original content of the Christian faith and of the doctrine of the church, or the changes they underwent in the course of history, but also to determine the truth which is contained in that tradition. All theological disciplines share in this task, but undoubtedly it is the special task of systematic theology, and to the degree that the question of the truth content in the documents of the Christian tradition is dealt with in biblical exegesis and in church history, those disciplines share in the special task of systematic theology.

The content of truth that is inherent in the documents of the tradition has to be determined again and again, because in each historical situation a new effort is needed to distinguish the truth of the gospel and of the dogma of the church from the evanescent forms of language and thought that at one time served to express such abiding truth. To make that distinction is possible only in terms of one's own thought and language, rooted in a contemporary setting. Therefore, the task of distinguishing in a particular traditional assertion the core of truth from the passing forms of language and thought arises again and again. In each historical epoch, systematic theology has to be done all over again. And yet, the task is always the same, and the truth which systematic theology tries to reformulate should recognizably be the same truth that had been intended under different forms of language and thought in the great theological systems of the past and in the teaching of the church throughout the ages.

The task of the theologian in relation to the traditional language of Christian teaching is a critical one as well as a systematic one. It has to be critical, because the distinction has to be made between what is historically relative in the traditional teaching and what is its abiding core. This task arises even in biblical exegesis, because the biblical writings are also historical documents. Therefore, time and again the substantial content of the biblical witness has to be reformulated. But the truth content of traditional teaching cannot be determined in dealing with details only. It needs systematic presentation. Systematic presentation is itself a test of the truth claims of each of the specific assertions that enter into a comprehensive account. The reason is that truth itself is systematic, because coherence belongs to the nature of truth. Therefore, the attempt at systematic presentation is intimately related to the concern for the truth that is searched for in the investigation of traditional teaching.

The most illuminating example of the task of systematic theology is provided by the doctrine of God. It is also the most comprehensive subject of systematic theology. If we take the title of systematic theology literally, it promises a systematic treatment of the doctrine of God.

In the context of Western culture, even today the word "God" is almost exclusively used in the singular. One may or may not believe in God or in "a" God; one may refer to "God" as a human projection or myth; but it is always (or almost always) the one God who is talked about. Such a way of using the word "God" implies as its semantic minimum the idea of power on which all finite reality depends. In another way, the same idea is expressed in the minimal description that the word "God" refers to a power that determines everything. Such a minimal description does not provide a full concept of God. It does not say what kind of power or determination it is that is referred to, whether it is a power of natural force or of vengeance or of arbitrary decree or of justice or of love. Answers to this question yield different concepts of God. In any event, however, the word "God" refers to a power. A God without power is no God at all, although that power need not

8

be violent; it may work by way of persuasion. God may be personal or, like Spinoza's God, impersonal. Although the God of the Bible is certainly personal, this is not necessarily a requirement of the idea of God in general, though the word "God," because of its religious origin, carries personal connotations. In any event there has to be some kind of power. Even the gods of polytheism are conceived as powers. In the case of the one God, there is only one such power, and accordingly all finite reality must be understood as depending on it. One may raise the question, then, whether the idea of God as only one implies that his power be unlimited, except for the requirement of consistency with his own divine nature. If the oneness of God implies the absence of any but self-imposed forms of limitation, the consistency of the word "God" in philosophies like that of Alfred North Whitehead is cast in doubt, because the one God is thought to be limited by the existence of a world which is not his creation and by its creativity.

So much for the notion of God as only one. Now, the idea of God as determining all finite reality involves that no finite reality can be understood in its depth without reference to God. For practical purposes, there may be descriptions of the world of finite things and even of human beings that abstract from their dependence on God, although the Christian faith affirms that relation to God as constitutive of their existence. If talk about God has any claim to truth, however, it must be possible to show that secular descriptions of reality are indeed abstracting from the fullness of its nature. It may be the case that the fullness of reality, even that of finite things, escapes our human capacity of insight so that we cannot obtain exact and precise knowledge except for the abstract models we construct ourselves. But even then it must be possible to uncover in the nature of things what it is that our abstract

9

models leave behind by the act of abstraction. It must be possible to point to traces of dependence upon God, if that is indeed constitutive of the nature and existence of an entity. If, to the contrary, the nature of things were thoroughly explained without any reference to God, it would follow by implication that there is no God. The very idea of the one God implies that all finite reality depends on him. Hence, such dependence has to be made at least plausible, if someone insists on the reality of God. And it can be made plausible only by entering into the arena of competing interpretations of finite reality.

The plausibility of assuming the reality of God cannot be established by simply calling on some particular experiences. It has to be made plausible that all finite reality depends on him, not only human beings and the course of their history, but also the world of nature. But how can that ever be achieved? The only way it can be done is to present a coherent model of the world as God's creation. This is precisely what theology always tried to do. Such a doctrine of creation cannot demonstrate in every detail the dependence on God of all the forms of finite reality. At its very best, the doctrine of creation could design a model of how the world looks if considered as God's creation, and of how we have to think of God if we are to speak seriously of the creator of the world. Actually, it is in rather general terms that theology in the doctrine of creation explicates the claim that all finite things, their differences and particularities notwithstanding, depend on God for their nature and existence. What theology can possibly achieve in this respect is always far from being adequate. But even so, the theological doctrine of creation should be able to nourish and substantiate the confidence that the world of finite reality is indeed susceptible of a coherent interpretation as being created by God. In such a way the doctrine of creation in its turn substantiates the truth claim involved in the use of the word "God."

But it is not only a systematic description of the world as creation that is required in order to substantiate an affirmation of the one God. If the term "creation" is restricted to the bringing into existence of finite entities, then it takes more than the act of creation to substantiate belief in a God who determines everything. If the God who created finite entities could not also sustain them, he could not be trusted as the one God in whose hand everything is placed. Since the creatures have their existence in a temporal process, they would have to rely on powers other than God for the achievement of what they aspire to in their developing existence, if God had granted them just the beginning of their existence. In view of the experience that finite existence is continuously in danger and seems to fall prey to the powers of destruction, the question is inevitable: Will the God who granted such existence also assist his creatures to overcome the evils that surround them? Or will the creatures in this respect be left to some other power? If so, the creator God would not be the all-determining reality. The discussion would move on the level of polytheism. Or could one imagine that God, existing as the all-determining reality, had created his creatures simply in order to watch them pass away? Such a God, certainly, would not be love. His creative activity would be capricious. Could that be consistent with other characteristics implied by the notion of the one God? In any event, Christian theology at this point goes beyond the minimal description of God in terms of an all-determining reality. It is the character of that reality and of his power that needs clarification here. According to Christian theology the nature and power of God is love. This is not first expressed in his sustaining and redeeming activity but in the very act of creation. To grant existence to creatures is an act of

11

love, if it does not serve another purpose but is itself the purpose of the creative act. But God cannot be at the same time loving and omnipotent (as one must suppose the all-determining reality to be) if he left his creatures to the powers of evil and destruction.

The old problem of theodicy arises at this point. It expresses the challenge that the idea of a loving and all-powerful creator God has to meet in face of the forces of evil and destruction that pervade the actual world. Therefore, beyond creation in the more restricted sense of the word, something more is needed to prove the plausibility of the assumption of God's existence; that is, the redemption and final salvation of the creatures is part and parcel of the demonstration of the reality of God. Not only is the doctrine of creation related to the task of substantiating the truth claims of the Christian language about God, but the same applies to christology and soteriology, and to eschatology, the doctrine of final salvation. It is only in the event of final salvation that the reality of God will be definitively established. The entire process of divine economy leading to that final consummation amounts to a self-demonstration of God's existence.

One could include all that in the notion of creation, because it is only in the eschaton that God's work of creation will be complete. If such a broad notion of creation were adopted, one could simply say that the interpretation of the world and of its history as God's creation substantiates the truth claim of Christian language about God. In any event these claims can be supported only in the form of a systematic and integrative interpretation of the world of experience, corresponding to the oneness of God as well as to the unity of truth which is expressed by the requirement of coherence as a criterion to judge any particular claim to truth.

So far, I have argued that systematic theology is necessary in order to substantiate the truth claims of Christian language about God. This task is met by attempting a comprehensive and coherent account of the world as God's creation, including the economy of God's action in history. To provide such a comprehensive interpretation on the basis of a Christian doctrine of God is more or less what has actually been done in systematic theology since the days of the early church, when in a context of Hellenistic culture Christians, especially Gentile Christians, had to justify their faith in the Jewish God and in Jesus as his final word. Explicitly, such a defense of the Christian faith in God by way of a systematic exposition of Christian doctrine as well as of the world of creation and history has been attempted since Origen's work on principles. This way of doing theology produced classical systematic work like that of Thomas Aquinas (who, by the way, was the first to state clearly that everything in theology is concerned with God). This kind of theology unites the doctrine of God in the more rigid sense of the word and the doctrines relating to the economy of God's action in the world. The two belong together like the immanent life of the trinity and the economic trinity. Therefore, everything in theology is concerned with God, so that God is the one and only subject of theology.

In modern times the systematic treatment of Christian doctrine not only continued but even acquired additional importance. Since the beginning of the modern period it had to face new challenges, the combined impact of which, at least in my judgment, gives even more weight to the task of systematic reconstruction.

The first of these challenges (and I shall restrict my argument to only two of them) resulted from the rise of modern science and the development, on its basis, of a complete program of purely secular interpretation of reality at large and of human life and history in particular. This development, which has been of preeminent consequence in shaping modern culture in general, tended to render a Christian interpretation of the world superfluous and pointless, at least in public discourse. The other major challenge has been the modern criticism of all forms of arguing by recourse to authority. This second challenge requires a more detailed discussion at this point, because it helps to clarify the specific function of systematic theology in the modern situation. It will finally bring us back to the other and even more awe-inspiring issue.

From classical antiquity to the 17th century, argumentation by or from authority had been perfectly rational. In many areas of thought, authority was considered indispensable as an educational means for the individual to obtain autonomous insight. In some areas, and especially in the realm of history, all our information was understood to depend permanently on authority. The only problem then could be whether a particular authority was reliable. But all this changed in early modern times. After the period of religious wars in early modern history, all argument by authority fell into disrepute. Authorities were understood as divided and as purely conventional. Above all, authorities are merely human. To follow the lead of authorities involves the risk of falling prey to prejudice. Authority and reason were no longer seen in harmony but in opposition, and it became the battle cry of modern culture to follow the light of reason, not the prejudices of authority.

In a special way, this applies to history, the former domain of authority. The modern science of history is based on a method of critical examination of all the relevant documents from the past, including what have been called historical "sources," and modern history aims at an autonomous reconstruction of historical processes on the basis of such critical examination of the documents of the past. Historical knowledge is no longer considered to be dependent on the acceptance of some authoritative tradition. Even in the field of history, then, reason has been opposed to authority.

What is the impact of all that on systematic theology? Until modern times, the systematic reconstruction of Christian doctrine was understood to be based on some prior acceptance of authority, the authoritative teaching of the church and the authority of the biblical writings. In the course of medieval theology, the correlation between these two authoritative sources of Christian doctrine was increasingly determined in such a way that the basic authority was attributed to the scriptures, and in the Reformation the authority of scripture was opposed to the authority of church teaching. The latter was not completely denied, but it was considered derivative and subordinate. In early modern times, all such authority, the scriptures as well as the teaching of the church, came to be considered as merely human. Scriptural criticism began by producing evidence of the human, not divine, character of the biblical writing, diversities and contradictions in biblical reports, indebtedness to now obsolete beliefs about nature, etc. Thus in modern biblical exegesis the Bible came to be regarded as a collection of historical documents. Perhaps this approach does not necessarily exclude the interpretation of the Bible as inspired by God, but certainly it would be a very different account of the inspiration of scripture than that of premodern Christian thought.

The rise and victory of modern historical-critical exegesis meant that systematic theology could no longer take the divine truth as a guaranteed presupposition of theology. Traditional Protestant dogmatics had not been much different from medieval scholastic theology in assuming that the divine truth of the Christian doctrines was secure before the work of theology even began. Systematic argument was not understood as the arena where the truth claims of traditional teaching are judged, but only as the explication of the truth presented authoritatively in the inspired scriptures. To be sure, medieval and even Protestant dogmatics did in fact determine what was to be regarded as the true content of traditional teaching and of the scriptural witness. But the tension between this implication of its own praxis and the assumption of a presupposed guarantee was not perceived before the rise of historical criticism and the modern suspicion against any appeal to authority. Even in the modern situation, however, theology did not dare to stand on its own systematic reasoning in facing the question of truth. Instead, the principle of authority in its function of an a priori guarantee of truth was replaced by that of personal experience and belief. Theology was now conceived as the explication of the content of personal or communal faith, the truth of which had to be presupposed as a matter of personal decision. William W. Bartley pointedly characterized and attacked this attitude as a "retreat to commitment": It actually represents a retreat from the arena of public critical discourse of truth claims of all sorts, a retreat into some sheltered corner of personal preference. The impact of this attitude on Christian thought did a great deal of damage to the righteous claim of Christian teaching to be taken seriously as a candidate of rational discourse.

But theology does not really need to retreat to subjectivism. In coherently restating the content of Christian doctrine, the discipline of systematic thought can stand on its own without a prior guarantee of truth. Of course, most persons who engage in such an enterprise will be confident from the outset that some sort of Christian teaching will prove to be true. But such confidence is a psychological incentive; it is not part of the argument. In a similar way, the theologian may be persuaded by the authority of the church or by the authority of the Bible. There is indeed a spell of authority emanating from the Bible and peculiar to the Christian church, although not everybody might be sensitive to its fascination. But, again, such spiritual authority must not be mistaken for a basis of argument. It should rather motivate an effort at examining its truth claims. In the course of such investigation and examination, authority cannot function as an argument. In fact, it would ruin the argument if it were used that way. Anselm of Canterbury was more sensitive to that problem than most theologians of later periods have been.

In the discussions of systematic theology, then, in the sequence of its argumentation, in its construction of coherent models of the world as determined by God's action, the question of truth should be regarded as open. Of course, if it turns out to be true that there is a God, that Jesus is risen, and that everything is in his hand, then this has been true all along. It does not depend on the effort of the theologian. Presumably, this was the most profound reason to attribute to some authority prior to theological reasoning the power to guarantee the divine truth. But the scriptures themselves tell us that the universal recognition of God's glory will not occur before the eschaton. Until then, the truth of his revelation will continue to be in dispute. Therefore, our knowledge is imperfect, as Paul says (1 Cor. 13:9), and this applies to theological knowledge in the first place. We are called to accept this situation and not to demand a final guarantee of truth before we even start to think. The modern criticism of authoritarian argument on the one hand, and the criticism of the retreat to subjective commitment on the other, have caused many theologians to surrender Christian apologetics and dogmatics, to surrender even the Christian truth claims themselves, and to turn to what are considered "relevant issues" of the time. But there is no reason to lose heart and to sell out just because there is no a priori guarantee of truth. The effort at systematic reconstruction of Christian doctrine is even more needed than in earlier periods of the church, because now it should be clear that one has to deal with the truth claims of the tradition in this framework. The results will remain provisional, but that is in keeping not only with the spirit of modern science but also with Paul's understanding of the provisional form of our knowledge, due to the incompleteness of salvation history itself. To engage in systematic theology in this way is quite compatible with personal confidence in the ultimate truth of the Christian doctrine, even more so than on the basis of a prior commitment to authority. A Christian should be ready to leave it to God himself to prove definitively his reality, and he or she should be content to perceive but vaguely and to adumbrate the infinite wealth of the truth of God. But certainly, we need to be reassured of that truth, and precisely there is the place for systematic theology.

To do systematic theology in such a way is not confined to the task of restating the traditional doctrine in view of contemporary insights in the fields of biblical exegesis and doctrinal history as well as in the secular disciplines. It should be an effort in constructive thought in order to exemplify how the God of the Bible can be understood as creator and Lord of all reality. Therefore, theological systematics must be concerned to integrate into its own synthesis the wealth of insight gained by the secular disciplines into the mysteries of nature, of human life and history. In a strict sense, it is only by way of such an integration of secular insight into theological systematics that the truth claims of the traditional doctrine can be restated. But such an integration of the secular disciplines' achievements into theology cannot consistently take place in the form of a selective transfer of some isolated results. It requires a critical reflection upon the methodical framework of the research done in those disciplines. The transposition of details into the framework of theology will consequently take the form of a critical transformation that nevertheless must remain accountable to the standards of those secular disciplines. It will not be possible to do this without creating new dispute and controversy. But the systematic theologian must not shy away from interdisciplinary controversy. It can open our eyes to see new possibilities on both sides. Controversy is far better than unrelated coexistence, because in controversy we are still concerned for the truth, which is only one. The prospect of general agreement may be somewhat dim, although the bold outlines of some agreed synthesis may become visible once in a while. The dangers of dilettantism are always close at hand. But then even in theology the excitement of systematically exploring the truth of God must not be mistaken for having that truth itself at our disposal.

2

Problems of a Christian Doctrine of God

In theology, the concept of God can never be simply one issue among others. It is the central issue, around which everything else is organized. If you take away that one issue nothing would be left to justify the continuation of that special effort that we call "theology." The teaching of Jesus and his history might at best be remembered as a somewhat eccentric contribution to the cultural history of humankind. But, without the reality of God, Jesus' teaching would be deprived of its core. The same is true of the church, though churches might continue as institutions that offer cheap substitutes for psychotherapy and occasions for moralistic advocacy and exhortation. The reality of God is crucial if one is serious in talking about a specific calling of the church as well as of a special task assigned to theology. Therefore, the concept of God cannot be exchanged for other concepts. It needs interpretation, but it is not a metaphor for something else, nor a symbol to express the changing desires of our human hearts, though certainly an

21

entire dimension of what it means to be human falls into oblivion where the word "God" disappears.

The contemporary situation of doing theology is charac- terized by the fact that in the world of secular culture the word "God" is not taken for granted, or if so, it is taken as a token of religious language, valid only within the enclave of religious discourse. The word is not self-evident as pointing to the ultimate reality that embraces, governs, judges, and explains everything else. The spirit of secularism keeps in suspense whether there is any such ultimate reality, though the secularist may be ready to respect ultimate concerns of people or what people pretend to be their ultimate concerns. In fact, to the various forms of secularism, human beings and their society count as ultimate reality. That hidden idolatry of secularism testifies to the fact that one cannot easily get rid of the issue of God. But secularism wants to persuade everybody that this issue is dead. Unfortunately, the credulity among religious people is such that not a few of them believe this to be the case, at least in the realm of public discourse, although the joke of making the "death of God" into a theological slogan turned out to be a passing fad.

A more serious problem is that many in the clergy seem to feel insecure about the reality of God, and consequently they are even more desperate to adapt their message to the changing mood of the time. Instead, the idolatries of secular culture should be exposed. Within the setting of a secularist culture it is even more important than in a religiously informed culture to urge the ultimate reality of God upon the hearts and minds of the people, and there are no other agents to do it than the preacher and the theologian. To insist upon the ultimate reality of God and its rightful claims upon our lives is to compensate for the basic deficiency in secular culture rather than to comply with its spirit. This does not require, however, some paradoxical decision. To the contrary, what is needed is enlightenment, a bringing to light of what has been suppressed by the prejudices of a secularist age.

Thus the theologian is called to restate the doctrine of God in terms of rational argument. It is not an easy task, for several reasons. First, the concept of God which was developed by medieval and early modern theology in close contact with classical metaphysics is in need of rather radical revision. Though the constructive theories of modern atheists and the details of the arguments they developed to establish their point were not particularly strong, the underlying criticism of the classical concept of God contained important elements of truth. Therefore, a revision of the classical theological and metaphysical language about God is inevitable. The second main difficulty that the theological effort at reconstructing the Christian doctrine of God has to meet is the desolate state of metaphysics in modern philosophy. In reassessing the classical theological doctrine of God, it would be helpful to have a critical but not entirely negative discussion of the great metaphysical tradition of philosophy, including the philosophical doctrine of God, to relate to. But with a few exceptions, modern philosophers have chosen to turn away from metaphysical questions. To put it more precisely, they ceased to occupy themselves with metaphysical issues in a constructive spirit. The schools of language analysis simply hoped to get rid of the burden of metaphysics by uncovering the suspected mistakes in the use of language that supposedly led to metaphysical ideas. This goal, on the judgment of important philosophers from the analytical schools themselves, has never been obtained. But still the problems and issues of the metaphysical tradition are rarely discussed in contemporary philosophy except in terms of historical study. There is little effort at critically reappropriating the metaphysical heritage to contemporary thought, though increasingly philosophers seem to feel that something like that is necessary. Thus theologians cannot take recourse to much philosophical assistance in wrestling with the metaphysical implications of the classical doctrine of God when they embark on the task of its critical reconstruction.

There were a few exceptions, of course, from the general trend away from metaphysics in post-idealist philosophy. The most important one has been process philosophy since it was created by Henri Bergson and especially in the form it took in the Whiteheadian system. It is understandable, therefore, that some theologians, in facing the task of a revised doctrine of God, turned to process philosophy for help. Others, like John Macquarrie, took recourse to Heidegger, although Heidegger rejected the tradition of philosophical theology almost as uncompromisingly as the language analysts did. In my own view, much more is necessary. First, the theologian should not rely too heavily on a particular philosophical system, but she or he should critically participate in the dialog of contemporary philosophy with the metaphysical tradition. The theologian must form his or her own judgments on the problems involved in this task and on the conclusions drawn by different contemporary philosophers. Even in the case of Whitehead, the use of the metaphysical tradition is highly selective and personal. The theologian should not take over Whitehead's or Heidegger's systematic conclusions without entering himself or herself into the dialog with the philosophical tradition.

The reason I emphasize this aspect of the task of systematic theology and especially its importance in discussing the concept of God is that in modern theology it has often been disregarded or even openly dismissed, to the detriment of the intellectual seriousness of the theological argument. Certainly, a Christian theological doctrine of God cannot be identical with a purely metaphysical argument that abstracts from any particular religious perspective. Nevertheless, in the entire history of the Christian doctrine of God, metaphysical considerations were allowed to exercise a critical function in relation to theology, critical as far as rational plausibility was concerned. Patristic and scholastic theologians, but also the representative figures of classical Protestant dogmatics, tried to meet the intellectual standards of philosophical argument in this field, even when they criticized particular philosophical assumptions, as the theologian indeed must do. The whole issue has been blurred in modern theology by a rather vague use of the title "natural theology" in terms of what should be avoided in decent theological thought. The rejection of "natural theology" has served as an excuse for not entering seriously at all into the dialog with philosophy. But to engage in critical dialog with the tradition of philosophical theology is not to do what is called "natural theology," but serves the critical examination of theological language. The less attention has been paid to this requirement, the more subjective and irrational theological language has become, even if the subjectivism simply consists in taking over traditional formulas and phrases without sufficient awareness of their implications.

In turning to the issues of a revised doctrine of God, let me start by recalling Paul Tillich, who was more alert to the problems of the traditional doctrine of God than most theologians of his generation. I confine myself to just two points. The first concerns Tillich's dislike for the idea of a purely transcendent God. Tillich was not a pantheist. He emphasized the otherness of God in contrast to all finite beings. But he knew that imagining God as a *merely* transcendent being *also*

25

mistakes him for a finite reality. He preferred to speak of God as the "infinite and inexhaustible depth and ground of all being."[1] This image of depth became famous, especially through Bishop John A. T. Robinson, who contrasted it with the traditional image of a God "up there," who would only relate extrinsically to the world. Bishop Robinson combined the image of God in the "depth" of our lives with the ideas of Dietrich Bonhoeffer, who in his *Letters and Papers from Prison* spoke of God who is transcendent "in the midst of our life."[2] The problem with these proposals was that neither Tillich nor Robinson could account properly for the *personal* character of the divine reality as Christian tradition conceived of it. Personal encounter involves an element of over-againstness that suggests transcendence. Tillich could have done more justice to this issue if he had taken the doctrine of the trinity more seriously than he did. John Robinson correctly recalled that classical Christian theology dealt with the personal character of God in the doctrine of the trinity. The Christian faith does not speak of God as one person but rather as three persons.[3] The divine essence as such was not conceived as person. The one God is personal only with regard to the concreteness of his trinitarian life in the interactions of Father, Son, and Spirit. Unfortunately, neither Robinson nor Tillich explored the significance of this trinitarian doctrine for the Christian understanding of monotheism. Hence their account of God as depth and ground of all being remained somewhat shallow, and the personal connotation of the very word "God" came to sound like a mere metaphor.

---

1. P. Tillich, *The Shaking of the Foundations* (1948), p. 57.
2. J. A. T. Robinson, *Honest to God* (1963), pp. 22-23; cf. pp. 53ff.
3. Ibid., pp. 39-40, with reference to C. C. J. Webb, *God and Personality* (1919).

It is well known that according to Tillich the only non-symbolic proposition regarding God is that God is "being," not "a being," but "being" in the sense of the power to be. Tillich rejected the conception of God as "a" being, even the highest being, and therefore also the notion of God as the highest personal being. He explicitly stated that "the protest of atheism against such a highest person is correct."[4] He considered any notion of God in terms of a being alongside other beings and in distinction from them as almost idolatrous, because it seemed to mistake God for one of the finite objects that we encounter in the world. Tillich knew that his argument was to some degree in continuity with one important strand of traditional Christian theology, that is, with Thomas Aquinas's notion of God as "being itself" (*ipsum esse*)[5] in distinction from all finite beings. Tillich was also under the influence of Heidegger's doctrine of "being as such," in sharp contrast to any particular being. In the case of Heidegger, however, the expression "being as such" was meant to exclude any idea of God, because any God — according to Heidegger — would be "a being." Tillich did not address this issue, nor did Macquarrie later on. Neither of them mentioned that the case of Thomas Aquinas was very different, because he did not exclude every notion of "a" being from the idea of God, but only those where the act to be comes as something additional to complement the particular essence of a thing. What is different in the case of God, according to Thomas Aquinas, is not that he has no essence at all, but that his being and essence are one. Therefore, Thomas Aquinas could still speak of God as the highest being. This formulation was not a deplorable mistake or a lack of

---

4. P. Tillich, *Systematic Theology,* I (1953), p. 271.
5. Thomas Aquinas, *Summa theologica,* I, q.13 a.11.

radicalism, but it indicates the superior sophistication of Thomas Aquinas over both Tillich and Macquarrie. As long as one wants to distinguish the divine reality from finite beings, it is logical to call God something in distinction from others, and that involves conceiving of God as "a" being. It is only at the price of atheism that one can avoid that. But is there not a difference between, on the one hand, being as such opposed to nonbeing and, on the other hand, particular beings? Indeed, there is such a difference. But that general quality of being is, at a first glance anyway, nothing but the most general quality that everything real has in common.

There arises, of course, the question of conceptual realism: Do our general concepts represent realities that are something in themselves and not only qualifications of actual entities? Thomas Aquinas subscribed to the medieval theory of conceptual realism, and therefore in his language a description of God as "being itself," subsistent being, made sense. But most modern thinkers suspect such language as hypostatization of abstractions, that is, treating abstract terms as if they were concrete realities by themselves. Neither Tillich nor Macquarrie even addressed this problem. Therefore, their talk about "being as such" must be dismissed as fuzzy language. But even Heidegger, at this point, is not above the suspicion of mistaking the abstract for the concrete, though he introduced his idea of "being as such" along different lines, not by simple contradistinction between beings and being but through the experience of nothingness.

The ontological language of being has the advantage of providing an all-inclusive survey of reality at large, and that is what has recommended its use in connection with the idea of God. The point in emphasizing the oneness of God is that everything real is related to him as to the source of its existence,

28

sustenance, and fulfillment. Thus the biblical God is the one and only God precisely in that he is the creator, sustainer, and redeemer of everything. The ontological language about God as highest being and source of being in everything else served to explicate this universal significance that is claimed in the very idea of the one God. But the ontological language served that purpose only in a very general and abstract form. Ontological talk about being and beings does not get very far in relating the concept of God to the concrete nature of the universe we know.

It has been the merit of process philosophy that it allows for describing much more concretely the cosmological function inherent in the idea of God. The Whiteheadian form of process metaphysics especially stands out as a rare example in contemporary philosophy of a philosophy of nature that assigns a place of basic importance to the idea of God in describing the world of nature and is capable of being related to the work of modern science. Though most contemporary philosophers remain skeptical, it is understandable that process metaphysics enjoys considerable prestige with many theologians. If one moves within that framework, assertions about God are no longer based merely on human subjectivity and on a decision of faith, but once again concern the nature of the universe and assign human beings their place within a cosmic order that is governed by God.

The problem with process theology, however, is that it does not allow for a concept of creation. The Whiteheadian God is but a partial factor in the constitution of actual existence, which is basically conceived as self-constitutive. Therefore, the God of Whitehead is not the biblical creator God. Furthermore, the Whiteheadian God is one actual entity among others, though distinguished from them by being everlasting. According to this philosophy all actual reality is finite, even God. Its picture of the universe is that of a pluralism of finite realities. But the very notion of a finite reality seems to presuppose infinity, an infinite horizon within which it becomes possible to determine the particular by distinguishing it from others. Since "finite" refers to what is limited, the activity of limiting and distinguishing one reality from another is bound up with the concept of finitude, and in distinguishing something from something else there is always presupposed an encompassing field within which all those differences occur. For this reason Descartes in his Third Meditation asserted the priority of the infinite over everything finite. This does not only apply to the operations of the mind but also to the world of nature, where the field has priority over every particular, where bodily phenomena have to be accounted for as manifestations of the universal field.

In relating the concept of God to the priority of the infinite over everything finite, Descartes followed the tradition of Christian metaphysics. Ever since Gregory of Nyssa the Christian doctrine of God conceived of God's nature as infinite. In this way, in contrast to Aristotelian and Platonic metaphysics, it accounted for the biblical intuition of a radical otherness of God, unattainable to all creatures, an otherness expressed primarily through the idea of holiness. In his transcendence beyond everything finite, God is holy, and it is precisely because of such transcendence that he is not bound to any place "up there" or "out there," but can also be present within the world of finite realities. The infinite God is transcendent in the midst of our lives, as Bonhoeffer wrote, because everything finite is constituted by the infinite, in the presence of which it exists. Paul Tillich also followed in the line of this tradition, and my earlier criticism does not apply to his adherence to the idea of

30

God as infinite, but only to the way he identified it with that vague notion of being. The argument of Tillich's doctrine of God could have been much stronger if he had consistently based it on the concept of the infinite.

I also criticized Tillich for the lack of personal concreteness in his concept of God as compared to the biblical language about God. In this respect, the idea of God as infinite is not better off than Tillich's concept of being, though it is more easily reconcilable with addressing God as Father and speaking at the same time of the same God as manifest in the Son and through the Spirit. Actually, the idea of God as infinite was introduced by Gregory of Nyssa in order to account for the Christian affirmation that in the Son and in the Spirit the same one God is manifest and present whom we address as Father. But in any event the concretely personal way of relating to God is made accessible only by revelation. Especially, it is not self-evident to call God Father, as Jesus did. Rather, it was Jesus' particular message of the nearness of God and of his kingdom that enabled him to approach the divine mystery in a spirit of such familiarity and intimacy. Therefore, in the Christian language about God, "Father" is not an exchangeable metaphor, though otherwise it may be regarded as a metaphorical expression on the same footing with words like "mother" or "friend."

In the Christian language about God, the word "Father" indicates that our way of talking about God and of addressing God relates to the same God whom Jesus talked about. Certainly, in order to function in such a way, the word "father" must also be correctly understood in the specific way it was used by Jesus. In the course of time, all sorts of misleading connotations have been connected with the word "father." Taken in isolation, the word "father" alone cannot fulfill the job of a criterion of identity with Jesus' way of relating to God.

Nevertheless, where the word "Father" is replaced by something else, there can be no warrant anymore that we are talking about and addressing the same God as Jesus did. In Jesus' teaching and prayer, the word "Father" came to function as a name, not a mere symbol. It was the only name for God Jesus used. And only in that way of addressing God and of relating to him did the unspeakable divine mystery acquire personal quality. Thus the personal character of the God of the Christian faith is bound up with the word "Father" as Jesus used it. The word "Son" as indicating a second "person" in the trinity is derived from "Father" as a personal name for God, and it is only in relation to the Father and the Son that the Spirit could be considered as personal too. Hence the personal concreteness of God, at least in the Christian tradition, depends on the name "Father." Therefore, the exchange of this name inevitably results in turning to another God.

Because of Jesus' characteristic claim to finality, his way of talking about God and of addressing God must not be seen on the same level as the guesswork of our symbolic language about God. In our religious language, no word is adequate in naming God. Therefore, human religion uses a great number of words and symbols. All of them are extrinsic to the divine reality which they refer to, and therefore they are exchangeable. It has always been the deep conviction of the Christian faith, however, that Jesus' way of relating to God was not external to the divine reality itself. That makes for its finality. Therefore, in calling God "Father," Jesus acted in the capacity of the eternal Son — eternal, because sharing in the eternal reality of the divine mystery whom he addressed as Father. Only by sharing in its eternal nature would he call its true name: "no one knows the Father except the Son and any one to whom the Son chooses to reveal him" (Matt. 11:27). The Christian confession of Jesus' eternal sonship was not exclusively based on his way of addressing God as Father, of course. The fourth chapter below will deal in more detail with the rationale for it. But it is closely connected with the particular status in the Christian tradition of the word "Father" as the personal name for God. Therefore the issue had to be raised here.

If, then, God is personal in the concreteness of the revelation of the divine mystery, how is the word "personal" to be understood? In what sense is God a person, or even a plurality of persons? This has been the most debated issue in the struggle of modernity with the traditional Christian concept of God. The critique of the idea of God as person lies at the roots of the history of modern atheism, and the protest against that conception of God was, as Tillich said, quite correct, though for another reason than Tillich supposed: It was correct not because the idea of God as person mistakes him for "a being," but because the concept of person, as it was understood in the theological and metaphysical tradition, violated the basic idea of infinity.

The problem is closely related to the traditional idea of God as mind, because "person" was understood as "individual substance (or subject) of intellectual nature," according to Boethius. While Aristotle like other Greek philosophers had taught that God was mind or intellect, medieval theologians argued that a being that possesses mind or intellect also possesses will. They invented complicated models of how the divine intellect and will interact so that the Christian doctrine of creation might be reconcilable with the Aristotelian concept of God as intellect, but they used this doctrine of God as mind and will also as a psychological model for interpreting the trinitarian dogma of the church.

The first major criticism of this conception of God as

mind was launched by Spinoza, when he argued in his *Ethics* that, on the one hand, the idea of intellect, as we know it in ourselves, involves so many limitations that it is irreconcilable with the infinity of God. If, on the other hand, all those limitations are removed, no sufficient similarity remains to speak in a more than metaphorical sense of a divine mind. Indeed, the activity of our intellect depends on some input from experience. Thus it presupposes something other than itself, contrary to the requirements of divine infinity. Furthermore, the distinction and interaction of intellect and will are bound to the finitude of the human situation, where the will depends on something given, that is, presented to us by the intellect. But what we intend to be is not immediately real; it has to be realized laboriously by choosing and employing means in order to bring about our purpose. All these characteristics are due to our finitude and cannot apply to God. Therefore, Spinoza rejected the image of God as a mind which operates by interaction of intellect and will. But since a "person" was understood to be an intelligent subject, the criticism seemed to deprive God of personality as well.

After a lot of controversy on this issue during the 18th century, Johann Gottlieb Fichte flatly denied God to be personal because of the limitations involved that contradict divine infinity. Fichte regarded the image of a personal God as a human projection, because the limitations attributed to God by that idea have their origin in our human condition. Several decades later, Feuerbach only needed to generalize that argument in order to let any idea of God appear as human projection.

The criticism of the image of God as personal mind is substantial. But its application is limited to the traditional Western doctrine of God. It does not apply to the biblical conception of God as spirit, because in the biblical languages

34

"spirit" does not mean "mind." In the Old Testament, the basic connotation of spirit is that of wind or breath. It is presented as a vitalizing power rather than an intellect. In this respect, it is related to the Greek word *pneuma,* but not to mind (Greek *nous*). In contrast to mind, it is quite attuned to the idea of divine infinity. The creative spirit of God in Gen. 1:2 is close to the intuition of an infinite field of power.

The notion of a divine will as it occurs in the biblical literature is not dependent on intellect. It is rooted in the experience of a power that demands something or urges one to do something. Thus the traditional Western image of a divine mind in possession of intellect and will is in fact an anthropomorphic image of the reality of God. This is the most important element of truth in modern atheism's critique of the traditional Christian idea of God. Christian theology should admit that criticism and receive it as a challenge to rediscover the authentic biblical awareness of the mysterious reality of God that surpasses all human images. In admitting this criticism, Christian theology will be alert, among other things, to the metaphorical character of biblical passages referring to divine knowledge. The ideas of a divine will and of God as spirit need not be surrendered, but they have to be reconstructed on a new basis.

How does all this affect the idea of a personal God? The criticism destroys the idea of God as one personal mind. But that idea was never an authentic expression of the personal character of God according to the witness of the biblical writings. The biblical God is personal in his elective will and action and as he is revealed as Father by his Son Jesus Christ. And because as Father he is related to his Son in all eternity, he is personal in eternity in the unity of Father, Son, and Spirit. In them, the unspeakable divine mystery is eternally concrete.

Therefore, one cannot have one God as personal without the trinitarian persons. This posits to theology the exciting challenge to develop new ways of integrating our conceptions of the one God with the trinitarian doctrine of the church.

3

The Doctrine of Creation in an Age of Scientific Cosmology

One of the greatest and continuing problems of Christian belief in God is presented by the difficulty of relating the concept of God to the world of nature and history, or more precisely: to conceive of this world as dependent upon God. The idea of God becomes superfluous if all things and events in the world of nature and in the course of its history, including human history, do not depend on God's action. The worldview of modern science, however, untied the bonds of dependence that related the world of nature to the continuous activity of a creator God. In the rise of modern science, this effect was not intended. To the contrary, Isaac Newton reacted against Descartes's mechanical model of the universe, because he suspected it would dissolve the dependence of the physical world on its creator. Newton's own physics was designed as a means of restoring the dependence of all natural processes on material powers, and ultimately on God. But the historical effect of his mechanical description of nature was, contrary to his inten-

37

tions, to render the physical world autonomous. Since the end of the 18th century this has become the dominant view of the world of nature, a view that profoundly influenced the presentation of human history, too. To many observers, the rise of Darwinism completed this view of the natural world and definitively excluded all reference to a creator from the description of the reality of nature. Though after the first shock theologians increasingly found it possible to combine the outlook of evolution with a Christian concept of salvation history, on the part of modern science the situation remained unchanged: Theological interpretations of the natural world appear at best as subjective additions to a self-sufficient and overwhelmingly successful scientific description of nature.

It is difficult to imagine even the possibility of a basic change in this situation. Since modern theories of nature are mathematical, such a change would require one of two conditions: Either God himself has to become an object of mathematical description, or all mathematical description has to be regarded as mere approximation to the true nature of physical reality, contrary to the widespread assumption that the very nature of things is mathematical.

I venture to opt for the second of these alternatives. Human intuition as well as physical reality always seem to exceed the formalism of mathematical description. One must not underestimate the subtlety and flexibility of mathematical description. It has proved adaptable to most intricate and puzzling data of experience. Yet its very precision entails its limitation: There is something in life which is not precise and systematically escapes that form of presentation. Considerations like this are required as legitimation for using ordinary language as an alternative way of describing reality, although such language notoriously lacks precision as compared to mathematics.

The assertion that there are inherent limitations in mathematical language is on safe linguistic ground, since all formal languages continue to be in need of interpretation in terms of ordinary language from which they were derived. On that assumption, we need not think that philosophical or theological assertions on the nature of things or on the universe of nature are necessarily inferior to their mathematical description.

A theology of creation is related to the universe as well as to the nature of things in particular. In fact, both these aspects always belong together. It is only in the framework of some general assumptions about reality (e.g., theories of measurement in time and space) that more specific phenomena can be described. It does not necessarily indicate unwarranted speculation, then, that theology in its doctrine of creation focuses on sweeping statements about the world at large. This is due to the fact that in theology the idea of God provides the point of view for looking at the world. The idea of God necessarily implies the comprehension of anything else. If there is one God — and only one God — then everything else is to be regarded as finite and as comprised within his presence. The doctrine of creation explicates this relationship. Therefore, it produces primarily general assertions about the world of finite reality. These general assertions, of course, have to be specified in due course, and only in such a way can they be substantiated.

Because of its close connection to the very idea of God, the doctrine of creation in all its parts serves as a consolidation and corroboration of belief in God. This function, however, is not limited to the question of the origin of the world. It comprises the continuing existence and emergence of finite reality as well as the prospect of its ultimate completion. In traditional theological terminology, the doctrine of creation does not relate only to creation but also to conservation, redemption, and eschatology; in other words, to the entire economy of God's action.

This raises an issue that has been much debated recently: Is the word "creation" to be understood as referring to the first origin of finite existence, or does it relate to the continuing process in the course of which ever new creatures emerge and take shape? Often this question has been asked in the form of an alternative between two ideas of creation, *creatio ex nihilo* (meaning the creation of finite reality from nothing) and *continuing creation,* which is not restricted to the beginnings but covers the whole process of the world and of each creature's life. But to treat these issues as alternative conceptions of creation is unfortunate. Both come from the classical dogmatic tradition. There, the idea of continuous creation was related to the act of conservation, which is to say that the preservation of what has been created once is in fact the continuation of the creative act itself. While the idea of creation in the first place denotes the origin of the creature, it also extends to its continuing existence, because the creature cannot exist of itself. It would be reduced to nothing as soon as the creative act would discontinue. Therefore, the conception of creation as creation out of nothing also applies to continuous creation. The use of these terms as if they would indicate alternative models of creation is due to an inadequate understanding of the classical terminology.

Nevertheless, there is a problem with the classical doctrine at this point. The idea of creation was indeed primarily related to the beginning of created existence, even to the beginning of the whole world as reported in the first chapter of Genesis. Continuous creation was not understood as a continuous production of new forms of existence but as preservation of the created world in its original order. Although in the case of plants and animals new individual creatures continue to appear, their species were thought to be fixed in the original order of creation. At this point, the classical doctrine as well as the biblical reports on the creation of the world remained dependent on the mythical form of explaining the world: Everything was imagined as having been established in the origin of time. It is at this point that the modern conception of natural evolution differs profoundly from the classical doctrine of creation. Therefore, the expression "continuous correlation" itself acquired a new meaning in modern discussions, because now it actually refers to the continuous creation of new forms of being — a view which paradoxically is closer to the biblical way of looking at reality in terms of a history of God's action. The element of contingency in the ongoing process of nature has become the mark of the creative activity of God in the history of the universe. The emergence of enduring forms and even of patterns of events now appears itself as a contingent fact in the course of that history.

How is God the creator related to this process? On the one hand, the act of creation, though it now spans the entire temporal process, has to be conceived as an act in God's eternity, that is, as eternal in itself. How, then, is such an eternal act consistent with the contingency of events in their temporal sequence? On the other hand, the act of creation itself has to be perceived as contingent if there was not a world from eternity. How, then, is the origin of any creature at all possible on the basis of eternity? And if it is possible to imagine that the eternal God resolves upon a contingent act of creation, how can that act be conceived as contingent without becoming capricious?

In facing these issues, the Christian doctrine of creation need not take refuge in psychological considerations, as the classical Western tradition did, as if we disposed of a psychology of God's freedom of will in relation to the ideas contained in his intellect. I suggested in the second chapter above that this type of reasoning was very anthropomorphic. The trinitarian doctrine offers an alternative approach, which builds upon the biblical idea that the eternal Son was cooperating in the creation of the world. The Son, then, in distinguishing himself from the Father in order to subordinate himself to his kingdom — as we perceive it in Jesus' relation to his heavenly Father in his earthly ministry — may be considered the origin of all that is different from God. The eternal act of the Son's self-differentiation from the Father would then contain the possibility of the separate existence of creatures. As the self-distinction of the Son from the Father is to be regarded as an act of freedom, so the contingency in the production of creatures would be in continuity with such freedom. In this way one could think of the Son as a generative principle of otherness, from which ever new creatures would come forth. The old Logos doctrine could be revised along those lines: While in the traditional doctrine the Logos was understood to comprise within himself all the ideas of God's intellect and therefore the plan and design of the world of creation, this function could now be reconceived in a more dynamic form, because from a generative principle of otherness, in generating ever new creatures, there would also issue a web of relationships between them.

Thus, a trinitarian concept of God disposes of resources to answer the questions that pertain to the contingency of creaturely existence and to the possibility of its origin from God. It helps to explain the related phenomenon of the multitude and variety of finite forms. It also provides a perspective within which the autonomous existence and life of creatures can be understood in relation to their dependence upon the creator. Here, the biblical tradition of the involvement of the divine Spirit in the act of creation is important.

I mentioned before, in connection with the concept of God, that the biblical idea of Spirit, especially as it occurs in the Old Testament, is not primarily related to the concept of mind but is of a more general nature. It evokes the images of wind and breath. Thus "spirit" is more appropriately conceived as a dynamic force, especially in terms of the creative wind that breathes the breath of life into animals and plants to the effect that, according to Ps. 104:30, they come alive: "When thou sendest forth thy Spirit, they are created; and thou renewest the face of the ground." The same idea underlies the account of the creation of Adam in Gen. 2:7: God "breathed into his nostrils the breath [spirit] of life; and man became a living being." Literally, it is the human soul that is here reported to be a creation of the spirit, but the modern translations are correct to interpret that phrase as "living being" and not in terms of a separate soul beside the body. Nor does the creator spirit consist of the power of intelligence that would produce the intelligent soul, which according to Greek philosophical tradition distinguishes the human being from the other animals. In the biblical story the spirit is simply the dynamic principle of life, and the soul is the creature which is alive and yet remains dependent on the spirit as the transcendent origin of its life.

The notions of spirit as well as of soul have been intellectualized in Christian theology under the influence of Platonic philosophy. The decisive figure in this process was Origen, who argued effectively against the Stoic idea of *pneuma*, which he charged to be materialistic. Origen's criticism was successful because of the apparent absurdities such a materialistic conception of spirit would cause in the concept of God who according to John 4:24 is spirit: God would be a body, could be divided and composed of parts, etc. In fact, however, the Stoic conception of *pneuma* as a most subtle element like air was much closer to the biblical language than Origen's identification of *pneuma* with intelligence. The fateful effect of this identification was that the relation of the divine Spirit to the material world and to the process of its creation was obscured. In addition, the divine Spirit was also separated from the created spirit, the human soul. Consequently, the divine Spirit could be reduced almost to a principle of supernatural experience and insight. In the history of Christian thought, on the basis of the reading of the scriptures, there certainly occurred reactions against such a restrictive interpretation of the function of the Spirit. Thus in Orthodox as well as in Calvinist theology the involvement of the Spirit in the act of creation has been emphasized. But in order to recover the broad biblical vision of the Spirit as the creative origin of all life, not just of the new life of faith, it is necessary to overcome the intellectualization of the concept of spirit. In order to achieve this, it may be important to be reminded of the fact that the modern concept of fields of force, so influential in the history of modern physics, is historically rooted in the Stoic doctrine of *pneuma*. The biblical idea of spirit as dynamic movement of air in the forms of wind, storm, or breath is closer to the modern scientific concept of a field of force than to the notion of intellect. It is only by derivation from the phenomenon of life that the act of intelligence is related to the spirit. The human mind, then, is a phenomenon of heightened life. In this sense, all intellectual life is in need of inspiration, an inspiration that in a certain sense lifts up the creature beyond the limitations of its finite existence.

All spiritual experience has such an ecstatic tinge. But the same is true of life in general. There is no living being that could live without an ecological context. Each plant or animal in a certain way exists outside itself in seeking its food and nourishing itself from its surroundings. When modern bio-chemists describe the phenomenon of life as autocatalytic exploitation of an energy gradient, such a description yields the same idea of life as an ecstatic phenomenon, a phenomenon which is surprisingly close to the Christian idea of faith as described in the theology of the Reformation: an existence outside oneself, realized in the act of trust in God. Could it be that, basically, faith is the uncrippled and untainted enactment of the movement and rhythm of all life as it was intended by the creator? Could it be, conversely, that all life in its self-transcendence is related to God? The psalmist says of the young lions that when they "roar for their prey" they are "seeking their food from God" (Ps. 104:21). Can we take this as a clue to the understanding of all life, to the effect that its ecstatic self-transcendence is primarily related to God and that in this way the range of its finite object (including the prey of the lions) is opened up to a living being? Anyway, the ecstatic self-transcendence of life is not something that is in the power of the organism itself, but arises as its response to a power that seizes it and, by lifting it up beyond itself, inspires life into it.

This is, I think, what the biblical tradition intends by talking about the creative function of the Spirit of God. We may add that in arousing the ecstatic response of life, the Spirit cooperates with the Word of creation, because it is the Word that gives each creature its particular form of existence. In doing so, the Word itself is empowered by the Spirit and the Spirit animates the creatures in raising them beyond themselves to participate in some measure in the life of the eternal God, who is Spirit. Such a statement does not carry pantheistic or panentheistic connotations, because the Spirit is always transcendent, and only by transcending themselves do the creatures participate in the spiritual dynamics. But the biblical language requires us to admit that the Spirit of God himself is operative in such a way in all creatures. This is different from being imparted as a gift as it happens in connection with faith in the risen Christ. Since the life of the risen Christ is thoroughly united to the Spirit, the giver of life, the believer in the risen Christ receives in himself or herself the source of all life and therewith the hope of his or her own immortal life. In this way, the Spirit is not *given* to all creatures, but *operates* in all of them by arousing their self-transcendent response which is the movement of life itself.

What has been said so far with special reference to living creatures can now be generalized to comprise all of creation. The Spirit of God can be understood as the supreme field of power that pervades all of creation. Each finite event or being is to be considered as a special manifestation of that field, and their movements are responsive to its forces. The concept of field lends itself to such a theological application, because it does not conceive of force as a function of bodies, but rather of bodies as dependent on forces. In the early modern period, the mechanistic conception of physics tried to reduce all forces to bodies or masses. This contributed to the expulsion of the idea of God from the world of nature, because God cannot be conceived of as a body. If all forces are functions of bodies, then God can no longer be imagined to be operative in the world of nature, because he is not a body. The introduction of the field concept by Michael Faraday turned the issue around in rendering the concept of force independent from body, though in the actuality of natural processes masses may have a decisive role in structuring the dynamics of the field (e.g., as happens in the gravitational field). It is the independence in principle of the field concept of force from the notion of body that makes its theological application possible so as to describe all actions of God in nature and history as field effects. This does not mean to physicalize the theological conception of the creative, sustaining, and redeeming action of God. But it does relate the description of nature in modern physics to a theological perspective. We need only remind ourselves that the field language of science is rooted historically in the *pneuma* theories of classical antiquity. This demonstrates the legitimacy of using field concepts in a more general way than in the formalized mathematical fashion of physics. The field theories of science, then, can be considered as approximations to the metaphysical reality of the all-pervading spiritual field of God's creative presence in the universe. It may belong to the limitations of the approximative descriptions of science that the scientific descriptions usually treat field effects as correlative to masses rather than perceiving the occurrence of such a dependency as an inversion of the more profound nature of field effects.

The theological use of the field concept in describing God's creative presence and activity in the world of creation does require, however, a theological interpretation of space and time. There is a particularly intimate dependence of the field concept on space, because it is hardly possible to imagine a field without any form of space. In the perspective of modern thought, space in its turn is dependent on time, since space can be defined as simultaneousness: Everything that coexists simultaneously is somehow organized in spatial relations. The relativity of simultaneity therefore accounts for the relativity of distances in space.

In the history of modern thought, a theological interpretation of the concept of space was a hotly debated issue in the late 17th and 18th centuries. Isaac Newton and Samuel Clarke regarded space as the form of God's omnipresence to his creatures. The German philosopher Leibniz took these ideas of Newton's as evidencing a kind of pantheism not unlike that of Spinoza. He argued that as a consequence of associating God with space Newton had to conceive of God as a body and as having parts. But Clarke retorted that infinite space as such is undivided and without parts. It is coincident with God's immensity. It is only with the occurrence of finite entities within space (i.e., within the presence of God) that space gets parted, and the geometric construction of space is based on that form of space by way of abstraction from all differences of content, as if space were composed of equal parts, the units of measurement. However, it is not possible to imagine any parts without presupposing already infinite space as an undivided whole. This argument was also used by Immanuel Kant and in his view demonstrated the intuitive nature of our awareness of space, while the theological implications were passed over in silence, since they did not fit in Kant's phenomenalist scheme.

There is good reason, however, to insist that the intuition of infinite space can be appropriately accounted for only in theological terms, as expressing the immensity and omnipresence of God. The case of time is similar. Plotinus already argued that the transition from one temporal moment to another presupposes the intuition of time as a whole or rather of eternity, since eternity means the whole of time in the form of one undivided presence. Nevertheless, the separateness of temporal moments in the course of their sequence may be considered as connected with the situation of finite beings in the flow of time. Only from the point of view of a finite being is the past lost and the future not yet arrived, while God in his eternity is his own future as well as the world's, and whatever is past is kept in his presence. Thus, God's immensity and eternity can be regarded as constitutive of time and space, and consequently it makes sense to speak of a field of God's spiritual presence in his creation.

If the notion of energy can also be related to this concept of spirit as field, the presence of God's Spirit in his creation can be described as a field of creative presence, a comprehensive field of force that releases event after event into finite existence. Perhaps such a view of energy can be justified in terms of an interpretation of quantum indeterminacy. It would have to regard the indeterminacy of quantum events as not only epistemic but real in the sense that in the microstructure of natural processes individual future events are not derivable from any given situation. They occur contingently from a field of possibility, which is another word for future. Such an interpretation of quantum indeterminacy substantiates a thesis which I tentatively proposed two decades ago in explicating the potential significance of the imminence of the kingdom of God for a Christian doctrine of creation: Every single event as well as the sequence of such events springs contingently from the future of God. This way of looking at the occurrence of events converges, furthermore, with the interrelatedness of time and eternity, because it is through the future that eternity enters into time.

It belongs to the essence of the act of creation that it aims at the autonomous existence of the creature. Such autonomous existence is possible only on condition of some permanence through time, and the first basic requirement for the emergence of permanent forms of finite existence — like atoms, molecules, and their aggregates — is regularities of natural processes. A second basic requirement is the expansion of the universe, as we know it from modern scientific cosmology, because cosmic expansion allows for temperatures to drop to a sufficiently low level so as to admit the formation of enduring creatures. Autonomous existence does not find its highest expression in sheer duration, however, but rather in some form of active self-preservation and self-organization. That is the level of independent existence that is obtained with the emergence of living creatures. Though other natural forms last longer than organisms do, living creatures represent an incomparably more intensified form of independent existence. Such intensified independence is bound up with the ecstatic form of existence that characterizes organic life. It is a peculiar combination of dependence and independence: The organism depends on its environment for its precarious existence and survival, but precisely thereby actively organizes itself.

Organisms obtain stability for their own life to the degree that they manage to control their environment. No other animal, however, has achieved this goal to such an extent as the human race. Since ancient times, notably so in the biblical story of creation, this has been noted as characteristic of human nature: It has the capacity of dominating all other creatures on earth. This human capacity, again, rests on a rather paradoxical basis. It is rooted in the peculiarly human ability to discern — to discern between objects, but above all to discern the objects themselves as self-centered entities, not simply as correlates to our own drives; that is to say: to discern them from ourselves and ourselves from everything else. Paradoxically, this ability of discernment empowers human beings to make themselves masters of their world. That is paradoxical because self-conscious discernment involves restraint, even self-effacement, which allows the particular nature of other beings to be perceived, but precisely thereby it puts the rest of creation to the service of humanity.

Since ancient times the peculiar capacity in human beings of self-conscious discernment has been regarded as evidence of their participation in the Logos. It has been considered so characteristic of human beings that the human being was called the logos — endowed animal or, in more familiar form, the rational animal. In the perspective of Christian patristic theology this also meant that the human being is the creature in which potentially the Son of God becomes manifest. And in a profound sense this is true. The Son of God, as he becomes apparent in Jesus' relationship with the Father, is characterized by distinguishing himself from the Father and thereby subordinating himself to the Father in acknowledging in the Father the one God and his kingdom. But what does that have in common with the human capability for self-conscious discernment?

Human discernment or self-discernment is primarily related to the finite things surrounding us. But it also includes the discernment of their finitude, and therefore it includes an awareness of what is other than finite. Thus, because the human being is the self-consciously discerning animal, it is also the religious animal. While all creatures are in fact related to God the creator, and the young lions seek their prey from God, they do not do so self-consciously. It is only in human beings that the relationship of the creature to God becomes an explicit issue. This, however, is intimately connected with the human capacity for self-conscious discernment.

Two characteristic features of human nature, then — religious awareness and the ability to dominate the earth — are both related to the discerning nature of the human mind. To keep them together in such a way as to subordinate the capacity for domination to the religious awareness of God is part of the destiny to which human beings are called. It is how the human being is described in the Genesis story as created in the image of God. To be created in the image of God is to exercise control over the earth, but to do so under God, so that self-discerning subordination to God is at the basis of all other discernment. To the degree that this calling is realized, the Son in his relationship to the Father becomes manifest in the lives of human beings, and since only in this way can human creatures obtain communion with the eternal God, it is also the full accomplishment of independent existence of the creature. Creaturely independence is not achieved by emancipating oneself from subordination under God, nor by putting oneself in the place of God as ruler of the universe. Such experiments are doomed, as we know, to disaster and death. But independent existence is intended for the creature by the creator himself. It is the freedom the Son enjoys in his responsive relationship to the Father. To embody this freedom in the form of the creaturely existence has been the aim of the creator in creating the whole universe, and the human creature is the particular place where this aim is to be accomplished.

4

Christology within a Systematic Framework

The Christian church is the community of those who by baptism, faith, and eucharistic communion share in the ministry and death of Jesus Christ and thereupon live in the hope for the new life of his resurrection. Thus the church has been called the "body" of Christ. That is more than a mere image. Few communities are built so exclusively on personal identification with one individual person. By way of such identification, which is the point of confessing Jesus Christ as Lord, the universal significance of Jesus' individual history comes to expression. The assumption of such universal significance is at the basis of the rise and growth of the church and of its mission to all humanity. Therefore christology is of basic importance to the existence and vitality of the church.

The universal significance claimed by the church for one human person, Jesus of Nazareth, has been expressed in the famous word of Acts 4:12, attributed to Peter, that "there is salvation in no one else, for there is no other name under heaven given among men by which we must be saved." Recently, this word has come under attack as a symbol of Christian exclusivism. But in fact it proclaims the core of Christian inclusivism, the source of the church's universal mission. Admittedly, it also excludes something — the charms of other saviors or would-be saviors. It does not necessarily deny salvation to members of other cultures and religious traditions, but it certainly claims that if those persons will obtain salvation, it will be through the grace of Jesus Christ whom perhaps they do not even know; it will not be through the power of their own religion. Is such a claim intolerant? I do not think so. It is perfectly compatible with an attitude of deep respect for the commitment of adherents of other traditions. The awareness of the provisional form of all our knowledge of truth helps to preserve such an attitude of human respect. But toleration is not indifference toward conflicting truth claims. To the contrary, toleration is only possible on the basis of a decision concerning what is true and normative. It is only on the basis of such an assumption that one can tolerate deviant behavior rather than being unconcerned. Toleration does not put conflicting opinions and attitudes on the same level; that is what indifference does. Indifference does not take seriously the conflicting claims. It is uncommitted and may not even be interested in the truth. Toleration is serious and committed but nevertheless aware of the provisional form of the human predicament, where people do not yet see the final truth in ultimate clarity. Therefore, the Christian consciousness of truth demands toleration of others, because "our knowledge is imperfect" (1 Cor. 13:9). But that must not mean that we surrender the truth claim that there is salvation in no one else. If we surrender this claim, the Christian church would lose its *raison d'être*. Why should one become a Christian, if Jesus were not the one savior in the world? To ask a Christian to surrender this claim means asking her or him to cease being a Christian. That should be considered impudent. But the Christian can very well be asked to bring forward this claim in a spirit of toleration. And, of course, he or she can be asked to give reasons for raising such a claim. That brings us back to christology. For the task of christology is to give reasons for the Christian truth claim that is the foundation stone of the church.

What kind of truth claim are we talking about? The statement that there is no salvation except in Jesus Christ presupposes another proposition: That in Jesus Christ — and' in him alone — the one God of the universe is present to save his creation from sin and decay. That is to say that Jesus is the eternal Son of God incarnate. In him it has become manifest how the creature can relate to the eternal God in such a way as to enjoy communion with him in eternity, beyond this earthly life, but already in each present moment. John Hick said correctly that as long as the Christian believes Jesus to be the Son of God incarnate, the conclusion is inevitable that there is salvation in no other. Unfortunately, Hick added that he can no longer conceive of Jesus to be the Son of God incarnate, because he considers this to be merely a symbolic or mythical expression. It is understandable that consequently he no longer holds to salvation only in Jesus Christ. Thus, the crucial importance of the question whether and in what sense Jesus is to be regarded as the incarnate Son of God is obvious. What are the reasons for the Christian claim that Jesus is indeed the Son of God and that this assertion is more than a symbolic expression of Christian attachment to Jesus?

We cannot find the answer to that question by simply looking at the evidence of how the title "Son of God" came to be applied to Jesus. Among the earliest evidence of this application is the opening phrase of Paul's letter to the Romans, where Paul speaks of the gospel of God "concerning his Son, who was descended from David according to the flesh and designated Son of God in power according to the Spirit of holiness by his resurrection from the dead" (Rom. 1:3-4). There is wide agreement among New Testament scholars that this phrase had been coined before Paul and was quoted by him as an opening statement for this letter. It relates the title "Son of God" to the event of Jesus' resurrection, while later tradition related it to his baptism or even to his birth. In Rom. 1:4 Jesus' resurrection from the dead is presented as the event of his designation as Son of God. But this act is related to his descent from Davidic origin. That meant that he could pretend to the throne of David, to whom the promise was given by the prophet Nathan that to his offspring God will be father "and he shall be my son" (2 Sam. 7:14). This secures the messianic meaning of the title "Son of God," which Jesus was given at his resurrection.

It is not considered likely that during his earthly ministry Jesus claimed to be the messiah, though his activities may have aroused messianic expectations. According to the dominant form of Jewish messianic hope, the messiah was to be a political pretender, and Jesus evidently was not. He even seems to have evaded that association, as his reaction to Peter's confession of him as messiah still shows in the present text of the Gospel of Mark (Mark 8:30), in spite of the apparent tendency of the later stages of the christological tradition to carry back the messianic glory into the earthly ministry of Jesus. He was, however, crucified as a messianic pretender, according to the inscription on his cross (Mark 15:26), and he may have been delivered to the Romans under that pretext. His crucifixion as messianic pretender, then, seems to be responsible for the combination of the title "messiah" with his name "Jesus." This explains why according to Rom. 1:4 the corresponding title "Son of God" was conferred upon him only in the event of his resurrection from the dead, when he was vindicated by God himself. Romans 1:4 would be unintelligible if Jesus had called himself the Son of God, as we have it not only in the Gospel of John but in some places of the synoptic Gospels as well, most notably in Mark 14:61-62 and also in Matt. 11:27. Therefore, the more plausible assumption is that phrases of later Christian origin expressing that idea came to be transmitted as words of Jesus himself.

So far, the systematic result from all this evidence seems to be in favor of those who consider the application of the title "Son of God" to Jesus as symbolic language. Even in the case of the successors of David envisaged by Nathan the word "son" seems to focus on the function of the king in representing God rather than on his person. Otherwise, the word appears as a metaphor. In the case of Jesus it seems to be even more obvious, since he did not literally fulfill the messianic role of Jewish expectation, that the messianic language was only symbolically used. But this first impression remains superficial. It is not possible, on that assumption, to account for the early rise of the idea of preexistence in connection with the title "Son of God." According to Paul, God sent his Son in the flesh (Rom. 8:3), so that he was born of a woman and lived under the law (Gal. 4:4). These statements were not intended as symbolic or metaphoric language, but were meant to say that the Son existed in God's eternity, before he became manifest on earth in the man Jesus from Nazareth. There must have been some deep conviction that the existence of the Son was from eternity bound up with that of God the Father.

Where do we have to look for the roots of such confidence? The reminder of certain Jewish roots of the idea of preexistence, especially in connection with wisdom, is not very helpful at this point, because at best it may answer the question of where the linguistic and conceptual means came from to express such an idea. It does not answer the question, however, of how such an idea could first arise in connection with Jesus. One could suppose that there must be a link to the very center of Jesus' behavior and message to bear the weight of such a description. Short of attributing the idea of eternal sonship to Jesus himself, there seems to be only one such link. That is the extraordinary intimacy in Jesus' way of speaking about God as Father and in addressing him as Father.

The saying from Q that "no one knows the Father except the Son and any one to whom the Son chooses to reveal him" (Matt. 11:27 = Luke 10:22) may not be considered an authentic saying of Jesus himself. But at the very least it reflects the experience and amazement of his early followers that Jesus in a unique way talked of God the Father. The repercussions of this are also observable in the Gospel of John (10:15; cf. 17:1-2). Precisely if that saying from Q does not come from Jesus himself, it has to be regarded as evidence of how closely his early disciples associated him as "the son" with the way he talked about the Father and addressed him in prayer. In any event, according to this word, the Son belongs inseparably to the Father, and the Father cannot be separated from the Son. It may be that only after the Easter experience could such a word be phrased. But then it expresses how in the light of that experience Jesus' unique relationship with his heavenly Father was perceived. That goes beyond a mere symbolic application of messianic predicates to the risen Jesus. The saying from Q about the exclusive and inseparable communion between Father and Son renders intelligible that the idea of preexistence could

58

arise in the post-Easter congregation and that Jesus the Son could be identified with the figure of God's preexistent wisdom and perceived as the eternal Word by whom God created the world.

One cannot put all the burden of far-reaching conclusions like that on a single saying, of course. The saying from Q has to be pondered in the context of what we know otherwise about Jesus' way of speaking of God the Father. The precise meaning of that phenomenon, however, and its implications can only be assessed within the context of Jesus' entire teaching. To call God "Father" was not absolutely without precedent in the Jewish tradition. It is only in the context of Jesus' teaching that the unique character of his way of talking about God as Father can be fully perceived.

If one looks for elements of correspondence between Jesus' way of addressing God and the general character of his message, the first similarity to be observed should be the proximity characterizing both the kingdom of God, the imminence of which Jesus proclaimed, and his way of addressing God as Father. In Jesus' message, the nearness of the kingdom was not so much the imminence of impending judgment, as was the case with John the Baptist, but a loving and saving presence of God as it is reflected in the providence of the creator for each of his creatures. This loving and saving presence of God, however, is open to the creature on one condition — that the creature puts its ultimate trust and concern exclusively in God.

This leads to the second point of contact between the general character of Jesus' message and the intimacy in his attitude toward God: Jesus' relationship to the Father is one of unquestioning subordination, a spontaneous and unbiased subordination that voluntarily arises from intimate acquaintance, but nevertheless subordination. It is precisely this kind of subordination that must have evoked the word "son" as a most fitting name. But now this subordination corresponds exactly to the attitude that Jesus asked from other men and women concerning their relationship to God and to his imminent kingdom: Seek first his kingdom and his righteousness (Matt. 6:33). Then all earthly needs will be satisfied as well (cf. Luke 12:31). The parable of the merchant who sells everything else for just one precious pearl (Matt. 13:45-46) describes the point in a very simple and forceful way. What Jesus called for in his audience was the same attitude that characterized him and qualified him as "the son." This is in keeping with Paul's teaching that the baptized and faithful Christians participate in the sonship of Jesus (Rom. 8:14ff.).

Thus, the divine sonship was not owned exclusively by Jesus. Others before and after Jesus could and can participate in that form of relating to God as Father. But in the case of Jesus the eternal sonship became incarnate in his person. It became his individual particularity, his personal identity. To him it was natural to behave in this way, while others have to turn to God from their earthly concerns and worries before they can live in that relationship. Jesus did not need a teacher to tell him, for John the Baptist, whose disciple he might have been for some time before his public ministry, had quite a different attitude toward the future of God: To the Baptist it meant judgment, which was accepted and anticipated in the baptism he conferred, while in Jesus' case the imminence of the kingdom meant the gracious presence of God the Father, if only we would open ourselves to his future and honor him as it is appropriate, that is, above everything else.

In speaking of Jesus as the Son of God, one should keep in mind the inclusive character of this title. It is the destiny of all creation that in the relationship of the creatures to God the eternal Son becomes manifest. That means that the creatures accept themselves in their finite existence as different from God and in voluntary subordination to him. In an explicit form, this can occur only in the human creature, because it is a peculiarly human ability to discern oneself from anything else and everything in its finite particularities from the infinite God. But in accepting themselves and anything finite in distinction from the infinite God and therefore in subordination to him, human beings do not only realize their particularly human destiny, but they also act in the place of every creature (see Rom. 8:19ff.). Unfortunately, human beings generally do not live up to that vocation, but as we learn from the biblical story they fall to the temptation of playing God themselves rather than distinguishing themselves from God and subordinating themselves to him. The human pretension of being like God (Gen. 3:5) prevents the eternal Son from becoming unambiguously manifest in our human personalities. Therefore, it takes a renewal of the human creature, a new Adam, to achieve what the human vocation has been from the beginning: to exist in the image of God. It is the Son incarnate who embodies that goal for which human beings have been created. In Jesus, therefore, the eternal Son has become incarnate for the benefit of all human beings. All of them are called to participate in his image, as they participated in the image of the first Adam. And while the first Adam, in his attempt at being like God, actually separated himself from God — from the source of his life — in the second Adam, the Son of God, human beings accept their differences from God and subordinate themselves to him as the Son does. Like the Son himself, in their voluntary subordination to God they will enjoy communion with God and consequently participate in his eternal life beyond their own finitude and death.

A personal existence that embodies the eternal relationship of the Son to the Father cannot be a private affair. Inevitably it entails concern for the sovereignty of God among all human beings and for their acceptance of God as their king and Father. Therefore, the earthly ministry of Jesus, his proclamation of the imminent kingdom of God, was an integral part of his own identity as Son of the heavenly Father. That ministry, however, did not relate immediately to the entire human race, but first to his own people, the Jewish people. It occurred only in consequence of his cross and resurrection that the ministry of Jesus issued in the universal mission of the church.

It is no longer uncommon in Christian theology to emphasize the Jewishness of Jesus. His message could hardly have emerged in any other ancient culture or in modern secular culture. It presupposed Jewish monotheism and was first addressed to those who shared the Jewish monotheistic faith. The point of Jesus' message was to remind his audience of the radical implications and consequences of that faith. The call to cling to the kingdom of their God prior to all other concerns, to the point that those other concerns would fade, meant to take seriously the *Shema Israel,* the Jewish pledge to the God of Israel. Jesus was not a founder of a new religion. He was a radical Jew. But in focusing exclusively on the creator God of the Jewish faith he was also very provocative. He disregarded the pride of a special chosenness, and he did not call on the authority of the Law of Moses (not to speak of its rabbinic exegesis). His own ethical teaching was derived from his eschatological message, especially from his perception of God's parental love. This was and continues to be, I think, an enormous challenge to traditional Judaism, even if Jesus did not actually oppose or break the law — less obviously so, anyway, than traditional Christian exegesis assumed. The laudable efforts of contemporary Jewish authors to rediscover the Jewishness of Jesus must not keep silent on this challenge to traditional Judaism. The challenge consisted in disregarding the authority of the tradition in favor of an exclusive concern for God and for his claim on his creatures. It was by no means self-evident to put the concern for God and for his kingdom in opposition to the rest of the religious tradition rather than to honor the tradition as securing human access to God. It is a challenge that asks for the nature of the Jewish faith itself. It would be helpful in Christian-Jewish dialog, if on the Jewish side that challenge would be admitted rather than treating Jesus as just one more example of more or less common Jewish attitudes. The challenge that came from the core of the Jewish faith itself also accounts for the resistance to Jesus in parts of his audience. However the Gospel traditions may be evaluated in details, the fact of such resistance should not be entirely dismissed. Nor should one reject every form of connection of such opposition to Jesus with the events that finally led to his death. Jesus was sentenced and executed by the Romans as a political pretender. But as this accusation was a distortion of Jesus' message and activity, he must have been delivered to the Romans under a false pretext, however one evaluates the details of the Gospel reports on his examination by Jewish authorities. It is quite likely that Jesus' way of presenting himself as the agent of God's kingdom while keeping aloof of the legal tradition could be taken as evidence of arrogating to himself the authority of God rather than submitting to him.

That Jesus was not accepted by the authorities of his people does not invalidate the fact that his ministry related to them. But his aloofness from the more particularist elements of traditional Judaism also included a potential universality and openness beyond the historical limits of the Jewish nation. This openness manifested itself primarily in the fact that Jesus did not become the founder of a Jewish sect that would separate the truly righteous ones from the rest of the people. The circle of his disciples remained open to all. The community of those who were accepted in the communion of the kingdom was expressed only symbolically in the celebration of the meal that symbolized the eschatological communion in the kingdom of God. The symbolic character of this action meant that others were not excluded as nonmembers. There was apparently a considerable degree of fluidity in participation. That changed to some extent when Jesus in facing his death left the symbolic celebration of the meal to his disciples as a pledge of continuing participation in his own presence as well as in that of the kingdom. Thus the celebration of the meal became the founding act of the church, and to the present day it continues in the center of its worship. Participation in the meal of the kingdom was now limited to those who would confess Jesus the Christ and Son of God. But implicitly some such confession was involved in the days of Jesus' earthly ministry as well, when Jesus personally participated and by his participation turned the meal into a symbol of the kingdom and of its presence. Even with regard to the church, however, it is important to remember that its community was founded on that potentially universal symbolism. The church is not a closed society. It is called to continue in Jesus' ministry and to further the kingdom of God among all human beings so that the eternal Son may become apparent in their relations to God the Father and make them brothers and sisters in their relations with each other.

Before I conclude this chapter, it seems appropriate to offer some reflection on the systematic character of the argument presented so far. It sketches out a systematic interpretation of Jesus' person and ministry as well as a reinterpretation of traditional christological categories. The key concept in the proposed scheme is the traditional category of eternal Sonship. But while in traditional christological terminology the concept of divine sonship was exclusively used to identify the person of Jesus Christ as the second person of the trinity, here the concept has been broadened to function as a more inclusive term. The Son of God is still considered the second person of the trinity, but while the Son became incarnate only in Jesus of Nazareth, he is conceived at the same time as being at work in the whole creation and especially in the life of human beings created in the image of God.

Such a broader application of the concept of divine sonship is required, *first,* by the biblical witness that all of creation was brought into existence and is sustained through the Son. Thus the incarnation of the Son cannot be properly conceived as a completely exceptional and supernatural event in the sense of occurring unrelated to the constitution of the creation at large. He came to his own, says the Johannine prologue (John 1:11). *Second,* there is the biblical witness that the eternal Son is the image of God, while according to Gen. 1:26 humanity was created in the image of God. Therefore, there must exist a special relation of the aim and destiny of human existence in general to the eternal Son of God. Conversely, the event of the Son's incarnation must be understood in connection with the creation of all humanity in the image of God. This has been done in the history of Christian theology as early as Irenaeus and Athanasius. But it has to be integrated with a *third* aspect: There is a broader application of the idea of "Son of God" in the biblical tradition both before and after the earthly ministry of Jesus. The dogmatic tradition took account of that by distinguishing between natural and adoptive sonship. The latter, however, was not always related to the second person of the trinity, but was taken as a kind of metaphor. Furthermore, the distinction may satisfy the extension of the divine sonship to include those who believe and thus participate in Jesus Christ, but what about the use of the idea of divine sonship in Jewish tradition before Jesus? One might say that the incarnate Son was *foreshadowed* there, for example, in the case of the Davidic king, but also in the people of Israel. That entails that the eternal Son was already on his way to his incarnation in the Davidic king, in the people of the covenant, even in human nature in general as created in the image of God.

If this is so, the concept of divine sonship becomes a comprehensive category without losing its special relation to Jesus of Nazareth. Since the eternal Son must be involved in all forms of God's relation to the world, this is not surprising. It is to be expected, rather, that it is not only in the event of his incarnation that he is related to his creatures. Perhaps in our theological tradition the idea of incarnation has been unduly isolated from the Christian interpretation of reality at large, and that may be part of the reason behind the recent criticism of that doctrine. In any case, the traditional doctrine itself requires a broader spectrum of relationship of the Son or Logos to the world in order to make the affirmation of his incarnation intelligible.

From the point of view of such a broader approach to the concept of the Son of God as eternal correlate of the Father, his incarnation and the advent of the second Adam coincide, because the incarnation of the Son is now seen as the completion of the creation of humanity in the image of God. This finally requires us to include in the emerging picture the church as well in terms of the eschatological future of human history, and in the present scheme this was done by relating the concept of divine sonship to that of God's kingdom.

The emerging synthesis is no more what I earlier called a "christology from below." But it presupposes and integrates that methodical approach. It surpasses it in conceiving of Jesus' person and ministry in the context of a trinitarian theology. That indicates the thread that runs through the chapters of this introduction. In particular, the trinitarian interpretation of creation functions as a connecting link between this account of christology and the doctrine of God. Thus there emerges a coherent scheme of interpreting the reality of the world and of human history in terms of a trinitarian theology. The coherence of such a scheme, its capacity to include and explain the details of our knowledge of reality, will serve as an indication of how far it approximates to the truth.

The sketch I presented is, of course, only one among several alternative models of systematic theology. It is characterized by its use of the idea of sonship as a central category. To some extent this corresponds to Paul Tillich's central idea of "new being." But Tillich's idea, like most of neo-Protestant christology (e.g., that of Schleiermacher), was not trinitarian. The present proposal is more closely related to Karl Rahner's view of christology and anthropology, though it differs from him in its account of the relation between trinitarian and incarnational theology. In the present model, the kenotic movement of the Son in becoming incarnate is understood as already characteristic of his eternal relation to the Father rather than involving a renunciation of his divine identity.

At this point, my model differs from Karl Barth's christological model, though I agree with Barth that within the framework of a systematic theology (in distinction from a christological monograph) the approach must be trinitarian. In

Barth's scheme, however, the transition from the trinitarian concept of God to christology is mediated through his peculiar doctrine of predestination which treats the Son of God as the only chosen but also the only reprobate and abandoned one. By contrast, in the present model the kenotic movement of the Son in becoming incarnate is taken as already characteristic of his eternal relation to the Father rather than involving a renunciation of his divine identity. In Barth's systematics the key concept is that of the Son's eternal predestination and abandonment. The creation comes into the picture only secondarily with the effect that the Son's humiliation becomes the elevation of the creature to enjoy communion with God. In the present model, the eternal sonship as such requires self-differentiation from the Father as a condition of communion with him. This idea explains the transition from God's eternal life to the formation of a creature radically different from God. It also comes to expression in the incarnation of the Son in the form of a creature, of a human person who accepts his difference from God as a mere creature like all the others and does so unto his death. This concept of divine sonship closely relates the incarnation of the Son in Jesus to an interpretation of Jesus' crucifixion and death as the ultimate completion of his self-discernment from the Father, but also of his unity with the Father. At the same time, in this history the destiny of the human creature to exist in the image of God by way of submitting itself to God is realized to the effect that the creatures participate in God's eternal life and glory by letting God be God. Thus the activity of the Son through the Spirit of God comprises the entire economy of God's action in creating, reconciling, and uniting the world of creatures to himself. In explicating the systematic coherence of this divine economy as manifesting the eternal life and truth and glory of God, systematic theology in its own way contributes to the commonly human task of glorifying God — a task that was never more urgent than in a world of secularist culture.